THE 30-DAY
HIGH VIBE
CHALLENGE

HOW TO STAY GROUNDED, CENTERED, AND IN HIGH VIBRATION

With guided audio meditations

ILONA YUKOV

SUNHOUSE PUBLISHING

Copyright © 2020 by Ilona Yukov

Library of Congress Control Number: 2020917557

ISBN: 978-0-578-23872-2

This book is dedicated to all seekers of inner peace and joy, and those who have been affected by the Coronavirus pandemic.

In the words of Mahatma Gandhi:

Your beliefs become your thoughts
Your thoughts become your words
Your words become your actions
Your actions become your habits
Your habits become your values
Your values become your destiny

TABLE OF CONTENTS

APPRECIATION

INTRODUCTION

Welcome to your 30-Day High Vibe Challenge! This will be quite an adventure! Hold onto your seats as it might be a bumpy ride at times, but it is sure to encourage all parts of your being to reach your desired destination! You can use this opportunity in any way it suits your personal needs. You will need a journal to do the exercises. This can be a simple notebook or a pretty journal. It does not matter. What matters is your commitment to doing this challenge.

Each day has its own theme. You can do a page a day or spread it out and spend more time on each day if you are not ready to move on. All the themes fall under one or more of these five categories: physical body, mental body, emotional body, energy body, and spirit body. I believe that it is important to care about all those areas to really feel grounded, centered, and live in a high vibrational state. Every day offers a new affirmation. You can change the wording to best suit you. If you feel resistance to how an affirmation is worded, it can help to begin with *I am open to*…(for example: Instead of "I choose to believe that there are no mistakes in life, just experiences," you could start with "I am open to believing…"). I suggest you keep the daily affirmation in mind, repeating it throughout the day. I also recommend you start looking at the exercises in the morning, so you have all day to practice and reflect on the theme. In addition, you will have access to guided audio meditations. Please note that they will be referred to in a particular order on certain days.

It is helpful if you can find a partner or friend to do the 30-day challenge with you, as it will help you stay motivated and allow you to share your experiences. You can also join the High Vibe Facebook community to share your successes and challenges at the following website:

Facebook.com/HighVibeChallenge

This book was written during the Coronavirus pandemic, which has been affecting, literally, the world. My intention is to help as many people as possible to reach their optimal self and help raise the vibration of this planet. I hope you find the information contained in this book and the audio meditations useful for wherever you are on your journey.

Warmly,
Ilona Yukov

ACCESS TO GUIDED AUDIO MEDITATIONS

Anthony Lepore of ViolaCello StageWorks created the background music for the guided audio meditations, and it is calibrated to 432 Hz healing frequency. The audios available are:

- Rooting Down
- Mindfulness
- Parts from a Place of Compassion
- I Am Peace
- Loving-Kindness from a Place of Compassion
- I Am Joy
- My Resilient Immune System
- Chakra Balancing
- Breathwork

All these guided audio meditations can be accessed and downloaded from the following link and are made exclusively for the readers who purchased this book:

HolisticWellnessNY.com/Audio30Day

Day One

Today's affirmation: "I am excited and committed to do the High Vibe Challenge. I am open to inner exploration and making new discoveries."

Intention Setting

This is an exciting day to start on your path! Today, I would like you to feel into your intention for this month and what you would like to get out of this program.

- How would you like to feel in your body?

- How will you know that you have achieved your goal(s)?

- How will you behave differently towards yourself and others once you have achieved this/those goal(s)?

- Are there any other changes you think can unfold?

I suggest you sit comfortably, close your eyes, and feel into this new you that you are getting to know. Journal about the possibilities that you are igniting. Notice if you are stopping your vision with "buts." Leave the "buts" at the door. Feel free and uninhibited when expressing yourself. After you finish journaling, do the following exercise from neuro-linguistic programming, which I call the *Circle of Potential*:

Start in a standing position. Imagine you are drawing a circle in front of you. In that circle is this new you, feeling centered, grounded, and happy. Notice your posture, your facial expression, and how you are feeling inside your body. Now step inside this circle. Close your eyes and feel all the sensations in your body from the top of your head down to the bottom of your feet. Stand with similar posture and facial expression. Stay in this space for a couple of minutes and remind yourself of this feeling throughout the day.

We will be using this powerful exercise several more times on this journey. However, it can be very effective doing it every day as part of your morning ritual, so that you step into the day that you want to create for yourself.

Every moment I shape my destiny with a chisel, I am a carpenter of my own soul.

—Rumi

Day Two

Today's affirmation: "I feel held and supported by the earth."

Getting Grounded

According to the Merriam-Webster dictionary, the definition of "grounded" is someone who is mentally and emotionally stable. A person who is grounded can handle a crisis calmly. The phrase "grace under pressure" usually refers to someone who is well-grounded.

Today, explore the concept of getting grounded and really feeling the earth supporting you. Getting grounded helps to build a stronger connection to the earth's energy. From this place of connection, in helping to bring your energy down in your body, a more balanced state of mind can be achieved. It is a technique to help support the nervous system in feeling calm and centered. Listen to the audio meditation *Rooting Down* to help you. Journal about what it feels like to be grounded after you complete it. You might also include what things in life get you off balance and how you can make time for even a short meditation as part of your daily regimen.

Day Three

Today's affirmation: "I feel connected to the nature that surrounds me."

Being in Nature

Today, we will explore being in nature from a different lens. I suggest picking a sunny day to do this exercise. Start walking to an area with some type of nature like water, trees, flowers, mountains, grass, etc. This could even just be your backyard, or if you are in the city, your neighborhood park. Start looking around yourself from a place of connection.

Everything we are made of is energy, and everything around us is also made of energy that vibrates at its own particular frequency. Connect with the energy that is all around you. You can connect with trees, for example, on a deeper level when you try to feel into its energy. I feel so much love energy when I connect with trees. On this walk, I encourage you to take your shoes and socks off and dig your feet into the grass (as weather permits). Hug a tree. Connect with the water if you are near a lake or ocean. Draw in the sand if you are at the beach. Really notice and appreciate your surroundings.

Returning to nature whenever you are feeling unbalanced can help you get more grounded and re-centered. Journal about what you appreciated on your walk today and anything else that came up in your experience, including any resistance you might have felt with some of the suggestions made.

Day Four

Today's affirmation: "I have (or I am open to having) a healthy relationship with food and enjoy connecting to food in a mindful way."

Mindful Eating

Part of feeling grounded, centered, and staying in high vibration is to really feel connected to everything around you. Today, we will explore mindful eating. This means connecting with the food and exploring it with all your senses. In general, our body digests food better when we eat slowly, chewing every bite thoroughly. It is also good to notice our breath when we eat. Are you holding your breath, or is your breath shallow? In between bites, notice and encourage the breath to move down into the lower abdomen. What state are you in when you are eating? Anxious? Relaxed? It is important to feel relaxed, as it can also affect our digestion if we feel anxious or unsettled. Are you talking a lot while chewing? You could be sucking air in while talking, which can lead to being gassy.

I suggest first blessing the food to connect with its energy and send gratitude for receiving it. Hover both hands over the food, and with eyes closed, feel its energy, send it love, and thank it. When starting to eat, take a bite, then place the fork down after each bite and chew slowly and deliberately, feeling all its qualities until it is completely chewed before swallowing it. How does the food feel, taste, smell, and sound as you are slowly chewing each bite? I would encourage doing this exercise with your eyes closed to notice if the taste of the food feels different or more intense. You might also discover that less food fills you up when approaching food in a mindful way.

If you have a partner, it might be fun to blindfold each other and feed each other different types of food from each category (bitter, sweet, sour, salty, crunchy). Have your partner guess what food they have in their mouth while they slowly savor it from a place of curiosity.

Journal about your experience. Did you make any new discoveries? You can also include how you can incorporate aspects of mindful eating into your daily life, such as blessing the food before starting each meal.

Mindful eating is about awareness. When you eat mindfully, you slow down, pay attention to the food you're eating, and savor every bite.

—Susan Albers

Day Five

Today's affirmation: "I lovingly connect with my body and feed it nourishing foods."

Conscious Nourishment

Food has the power to give us energy or deplete us. We are all different with what foods work best for us, and that might also change with time. So certain foods that felt good five years ago, for example, might feel different today. What is healthy for one person might not work for someone else. There are so many different types of diets out there—diets that are high in carbs, diets low in carbs, diets high in protein, diets low in protein, etc. Some people do better with higher fat diets than others. The point is, every person is unique in what works best for them.

It might be interesting to know that serotonin, a neurotransmitter responsible for many bodily functions, including keeping the immune system strong, also plays an important role in emotions and happiness. It is estimated that approximately 90% of our serotonin level is produced in the gut. There is more production of this "feel-good" neurotransmitter when the bacterial environment in our gut is in balance, according to a study published in 2015 at California Institute of Technology.[1] Therefore, it is important to keep our digestive system strong by eating unprocessed, nutrient-rich foods (preferably organic), which help keep a healthy microbiome environment.

Today, contemplate and journal with these questions in mind: What foods give me energy, give me a sense of alertness, and feel healthy for my body? Make a list of those foods. Then write down the opposite. What foods feel depleting, heavy, and don't feel healthy for my body? An entire book could be written on this topic alone, so don't overwhelm yourself. This is also a work in progress, and the more you connect with your body, the easier it will be to make this list.

Today's suggestion is to find a new recipe to cook using some of the foods that help you feel focused and energized. Use the guide below:

- Foods that help me focus and feel energizing for my body are:

- Foods that feel heavy, sluggish, and/or deplete my energy are:

- My action steps in eating more healthy foods that support staying in a high vibration:

Let food be thy medicine, thy medicine shall be thy food.

—Hippocrates

Day Six

Today's affirmation: "My body is my temple, and I honor it from a place of love and compassion."

Caring for My Physical Body

Today is about focusing on your physical body. Just like the mind affects the body, the body, in turn, can affect the mind. The research psychologist James Blumenthal has explored the mood-exercise connection through a series of randomized controlled trials. In one such study, he and his colleagues assigned sedentary adults with major depressive disorder to one of four groups: supervised exercise, home-based exercise, antidepressant therapy, or a placebo pill. After four months of treatment, Blumenthal found patients in the exercise and antidepressant groups had higher rates of remission than the patients on the placebo. He concluded that exercise was generally comparable to antidepressants for patients with major depressive disorder.[2]

Today, do something that gets your body moving. This could be anything from putting on music and dancing in your living room to going to the gym, going for a run, doing yoga, taking an exercise class, taking a brisk walk, etc. If you already have a daily routine, great! Ideally, it is good to combine both stretching and aerobic exercise, but do what works for you. Journal about what you are grateful for regarding your body and the amazing things it has been doing for you throughout the years!

Thank you, body, for...

Day Seven

Today's affirmation: "I make choices that support me feeling restful and energized when I wake up in the morning."

Sleep

The topic of sleep is important since a good night's sleep can leave you feeling energized and grounded. How do you generally feel when you don't get enough sleep, or the quality of your sleep suffers? I know I can feel irritable, cranky, sluggish, and frankly, in low vibration when I don't sleep well. The habits and rituals we carry out before going to sleep can make a profound difference in how we wake up. The following are habits, items, and tools that can be used to support good quality sleep:

- It is helpful when the bedroom is completely dark. Blackout shades do the trick well.

- Using an eye mask helps you get to sleep and go back to sleep, especially if you are prone to waking up in the middle of the night.

- Make sure the temperature is comfortable and on the cool side. Our body temperature naturally rises through the night, so we get hotter as the night goes on.

- Using a diffuser with essential oil can help you fall asleep; it can also help with breathing more deeply as you drift off to sleep. Oils like lavender, vetiver, and Roman chamomile work well.

- You might want to try using a weighted blanket if you have trouble sleeping peacefully. The deep compression can be very calming to the nervous system. Just keep in mind, especially if using it with kids, not to get a blanket that is heavier than 10% of the body weight.

- Structured time (going to sleep and waking up at the same time every day) is important, especially if you are prone to insomnia.

- It is important to turn off all electronics about an hour before retiring to bed. The blue light that comes through computer screens, TVs, and phones affects our physiology. Blue light hinders the production of sleep hormones like melatonin. Blue light blocking glasses can be really helpful in addressing this issue when they are worn at night. During the day, wearing the glasses can be helpful when sitting in front of a computer to prevent digital eye strain.

- If sound is an issue, try using a white noise machine. Now you can even get the sound through apps on the phone. You can choose between white, pink, or brown noise. I personally prefer brown noise.

- Journaling before going to sleep is helpful to write down anything that came up during the day, so you don't need to think about it at night.

- Doing meditations, breathing exercises or energy practices like Qi Gong can be helpful to wind down before going to sleep. Listening to *I Am Peace, Rooting Down,* and/or *Mindfulness* before going to bed are examples of meditations that help calm the mind and body. *Progressive muscle relaxation,* a technique where you are tightening a group of muscles on the inhale and relaxing them on the exhale, can also be very effective in eliciting deep sleep.

- To help the mind relax, one of the most powerful tools is using the Emotional Freedom Technique (EFT).

Emotional Freedom Technique (EFT), also commonly referred to as "tapping," involves lightly tapping with your fingertips on acupressure points that run along meridian pathways while you think about your problem. You incorporate language that first acknowledges the issue and then use positive language to release the emotional or physical pain it has caused you. It works to cut off the sympathetic nervous system reaction (responsible for our fight and flight response) and elicit the parasympathetic nervous system reaction (responsible for our calming response).

I have been using EFT along with other techniques in my practice for issues such as insomnia, panic attacks, anxiety, physical pain, and emotional pain with great success. Clients have even been able to get off sleep medications with the help of EFT tapping. You can explore it here: TheTappingSolution.com. There is also a wonderful app called *The Tapping Solution* that has tapping scripts for all sorts of issues, including sleep. The following website has more information on the science of tapping with research supporting its efficacy: ScienceOfTapping.org. The book *The Tapping Solution: A Revolutionary System for Stress–Free Living* by Nick Ortner and Mark Hyman M.D. is a great resource as well.

Today, the goal is to have the affirmation in mind while you notice your sleep patterns. Is your nighttime ritual effective? Do you wind down enough before going to sleep? Do you think you can find anything on this list that can be helpful? Journal about what you can do to improve your quality of sleep, if that is needed, and try something from the list tonight.

Sleep is the golden chain that ties health and our bodies together.

—Thomas Dekker

Day Eight

Today's affirmation: "I am committed to living my life passionately!"

Passion

Today is about noticing what is alive in you. What are you passionate about? What gives you that burst of energy and makes you want to get up in the morning? Journal about all the things that bring you joy and that you feel passionate about. Make time today to fulfill some of those things on the list.

You can write about what is alive in you for each category. For example, in health and fitness, I feel passionate about healthy eating and practicing yoga. In rejuvenation/self-care, I feel passionate about meditating. In relationships, I feel passionate about having deep, meaningful conversations with friends and my partner. In the area of career, I feel passionate about doing nutrition and life coaching to help people achieve their health and wellness goals. I also feel passionate about writing this book and helping people rewire their brains to get to a higher vibration.

Now, it's your turn! Look at the following chart to give you an idea of all the areas in your life you can be looking at. Wouldn't life feel amazing to approach everything from this place of aliveness? Can you feel what it would be like to bring the energy of passion into the things we do on a daily basis? Explore ways you can bring more passion into your life in the areas you feel are lacking.

Areas of Life
Fun/Recreation/Hobbies
Health/Fitness
Money/Finances
Cooking
Friends/ Social Activities
Community/Service
Career
Relationships/Family
Spirituality
Home Environment
Education/ Personal Growth
Rejuvenation/Self-Care

You can listen to the audio *I Am Joy* to help get you into this state of mind. Feel into this energy and carry it with you throughout the day.

There is no passion to be found playing small—in settling for a life that is less than the one you are capable of living.

—Nelson Mandela

Day Nine

Today's affirmation: "I notice my thoughts from an observer's position and choose not to identify with them since I am not my thoughts."

I Am Not My Thoughts

For the majority of people, most thoughts tend to be negative. Negative thinking can turn into a pattern in the brain where images, memories, and thoughts that surface help to reinforce the sensations in our body that negative thoughts create. Dr. Joe Dispenza has been a prominent researcher in the field of brain psychology and discusses the possibilities of the mind in its influence on behavior. According to Dr. Dispenza, from his book, *Evolve Your Brain*, we choose to repeat the same circumstances because of our addiction to the emotional state they produce and the neurochemicals that provoke that state of being.

The first part of changing our thoughts is awareness. Today's exercise is about noticing how many negative thoughts you have. You decide what is considered negative based on how it feels in your body. Keep a small notepad with you and make a small mark every time you notice a negative thought, without any judgment. You can also make a small mark of positive thoughts you carry throughout the day to really notice for yourself, from an observer's position, how your mind is functioning on a given day. Add up the number of positive vs. negative thoughts at the end of the day. This will give you an idea and increase your awareness to the state of your mind (obviously, it changes daily, but it will still be very revealing). Journal about what you have noticed. Is there any theme that has come up for you in the day about any particular emotion(s) your thoughts are evoking?

Day Ten

Today's affirmation: "I have the power to change my thoughts and I choose to think positive thoughts that serve me. I choose to stay at a high vibration."

Evoking Positive Thinking

Today, we will continue working on our thought patterns using concepts that are adapted from the book "*Loving What Is*" by Byron Katie. Byron Katie suffered from deep depression until she started to analyze her thought patterns and made the conscious decision to dis-identify with them. On the website, TheAgeofIdeas.com, she is quoted saying:

> I discovered that when I believed my thoughts I suffered, but when I didn't believe them, I didn't suffer and that this is true for every human being. Freedom is as simple as that. A thought is harmless unless we believe it. It's not our thoughts, but our attachment to our thoughts, that causes suffering. Attaching to a thought means believing that it's true, without inquiring. A belief is a thought that we've been attaching to, often for years.

In her book, she encourages people to ask the following four questions when negative thoughts arise:

Question 1: *Is it true?*

Ask yourself if the thought you wrote down is a fact or an opinion.

Question 2: *Can you absolutely know it's true?*

Use this as an opportunity to investigate and go deeper to find the answers that live beneath what we think we know.

Question 3: *How do you react when you believe that thought?*

What happens in your body? With this question, you start to notice a direct link between the body and mind. You can see that when you believe the thought, there is some sort of feeling of unsettlement that can range from mild discomfort to anger or panic, which would put you in a lower vibrational state. When you believe that thought, what do you feel? How do you treat the person (or situation) who (or that) you are reacting to? How do you treat yourself?

Question 4: *Who would you be without the thought?*

Basically, do you really need this thought, and do you need it at this moment? Imagine yourself standing in front of that person (or being in that situation), without believing the thought. How would your life be different if that stressful thought didn't enter your mind? How would you feel? Which do you prefer—life with or without the thought? Which feels more pleasant, more peaceful?

We have the power to change our thoughts and notice our thoughts as an observer. It is also helpful to ask yourself-what are other ways I can look at this situation? You can remind yourself that people react differently, even if they are in the same situation since our reactions rely heavily on our past experiences.

Byron Katie goes into another step that she calls the "turnaround." This looks at how you can look at the same situation from the opposite perspective. If I have a thought, for example, that my sister is too selfish, I would say the opposite for the turnaround and find examples (preferably three) of when she was giving. This would help release any emotions, like anger, that don't serve me. You can read more about her work in *Loving What Is* if you want more examples of this process.

If our goal in life is to be happy and stay in a high vibration, then what thoughts do we really need to entertain, and what thoughts can we do without? Negative thoughts tend to create a domino effect of more negative thoughts. A way to change that course is to bring up positive thoughts and images for at least 20 seconds. This helps to reset the brain. It also helps when you start using your peripheral vision (meaning while looking straight ahead, notice what you see on the sides as well). Notice the physical environment around you and name objects or things, like there is a brown table and colorful lamp, etc. This also helps to shift course.

Today, I would like you to notice and ask yourself the four questions that were mentioned when you come across thoughts that don't keep you in a happy state of mind. Journal about your experience with your mind today.

Day Eleven

Today's affirmation: "I choose to get out of my head and be 100% present in the now."

Present in the Now

Today is probably one of the most powerful lessons in learning how to stay centered and in high vibration. Being in the now is about surrendering to what is happening in your moment to moment experience without having an attachment to an outcome. It's about letting go of control of how things should be and being with what is. This is how we can get out of our analytical minds and be 100% present to the people, circumstances, and environment around us. Eckhart Tolle, a spiritual teacher who wrote the #1 New York Times Bestseller, *The Power of Now,* devoted an entire book to this subject!

Today is about making an effort to be present in the now. This means no multitasking! Neuroscientist Dan Levitan concluded that multitasking raises the stress response in our body and causes an increased secretion of cortisol and adrenaline (stress hormones). Moreover, multitasking can turn into a habit that can be addictive. The constant switching from one task to another creates a distractible state of never being fully present, which trains the brain to have a short attention span that can also affect your memory capacity.[3]

To help you with focus and concentration, listen to the audio meditation *Mindfulness*. You can also do the *Rooting Down* meditation to assist you with getting grounded. I recommend incorporating these two meditations into your daily routine. Try to be 100% present throughout the day today, which means focusing your attention on one person, place, or thing. When you notice that you are getting back into your head, use your peripheral vision to notice aspects of your environment. For example, if you are outside, notice the colors of the leaves on the trees or the types of buildings you are passing. If you are inside, notice the items in your house or the furniture to help you reset and get back to the present moment, without any judgment. You can also use your breath as an anchor, like in the meditations, to help you get back to being in the present moment. Journal about your experience today, being in the now.

Do not dwell in the past, do not dream of the future, concentrate the mind on the present moment.

—Buddha

Day Twelve

Today's affirmation: "I am not my emotions. I send compassion to all the parts in me that feel unsettled."

I Am Not My Emotions

Just like you are not your thoughts, you are also not your emotions. You *experience* emotions. You can observe emotions like fear, sadness, or anger as separate from you, without identifying with them. *Inner Relationship Focusing*, developed by Ann Weiser Cornell and Barbara McGavin, is a body-based therapeutic practice that focuses on noticing different parts of you that might make you feel unsettled and want your attention. *Internal Family Systems (IFS)*, developed by Richard C. Schwartz, is a psychotherapy model that works at understanding the mind as a system of subpersonalities.

Both practices are very powerful and can help people attain a peaceful state of mind. See the **Appendix** for further guidance to my own synthesis of parts work using some techniques I love, including *Focusing* and *IFS,* before listening to the audio.

Today, listen to the guided meditation *Parts from a Place of Compassion,* as we explore our inner parts. Journal about your experience and any feedback you received from your part(s).

Day Thirteen

Today's affirmation: "I give myself permission to release feelings that don't serve me. I bring myself back to my center and state of inner peace."

Letting Go

Our feelings are our interpretations of a situation based on our perceptions. Our perceptions of our environment are formulated from our unique past experiences and how we have made sense of our world, which is biased. Feelings such as anger, disappointment, shame, guilt, irritation can surface. It is important to notice and be aware of how they feel in your body. I know, for example, my body tenses and constricts when I feel angry. My breath becomes more shallow. My gut might also get involved and feel tight and constricted. This can even affect how I digest food. Other people might feel tension in their shoulders and neck. We all process feelings in our body differently. The point remains the same. We don't need to hold onto feelings that don't serve us. It is important to notice and acknowledge the feeling. Then let it go.

Two methods that can be very useful in letting go are *Emotional Freedom Technique (EFT)* and *Transcend Resistant Emotions (TRE)*.

The first is the EFT tapping technique that was previously discussed and can be explored on the website TheTappingSolution.com or looking into *The Tapping Solution* app. The book *The Tapping Solution: A Revolutionary System for Stress–Free Living* by Nick Ortner and Mark Hyman M.D. is a great resource as well.

The second is a technique that I developed, which I also find powerful and have been using it with clients and myself. I call it *Transcend Resistant Emotions* or *TRE* method. Follow these instructions:

1. **Feel in your body.** Sit comfortably and close your eyes. Feel into the uncomfortable feeling you want to release. For example: *I feel angry.*

2. **Welcome the energy.** Welcome the feeling and notice its qualities. What does the energy feel like? Is it spacious or constricted? Does the energy feel dense, jumpy, or stagnant? Does it have a shape or color? For example: *I am feeling tension and constriction in my chest, and it appears black in the form of a rectangle. It feels stagnant.* Be with this feeling in your body from a place of empathy and non-judgment.

3. **Give it permission.** Then give this feeling permission to let go. Sometimes, just being with the feeling can be enough for it to release. For example: Say to that energy (inwardly to yourself), *"It's ok, I give permission for you to release this feeling of anger."*

4. **Resource it.** Use the table on the next page. Ask: What resourced state do I need to fully let go of this feeling? Evoke the resourced state and send that energy from the top of your head down to the bottom of your feet, lingering in the area that gave you discomfort. For example: *I would imagine a time when I felt at peace and send that energy of peace from the top of my head down to the bottom of my feet, allowing it to linger in my chest (where the tension and*

constriction was). I would then imagine feeling compassion by thinking about someone I care about and send that energy of compassion from the top of my head down to the bottom of my feet, lingering again in my chest area.

Let's say you feel fear, and you want to elicit the feeling of safety. It is helpful to feel what it is like to be a baby being held by an adult who is offering safety and protection. That feeling of safety and security can then be brought into your body. You might need different resources or additional resources. See the guide below for some of the most common feeling states:

Feeling	Resourced State
Angry	Peace and Compassion
Scared	Peace and Safety
Irritated	Peace and Compassion
Frustrated	Peace and Compassion
Disappointed	Love and Compassion
Ashamed	Love and Compassion
Guilty	Love and Compassion
Numb	Joy and Passion
Sad	Joy and Gratitude
Disconnected or Lonely	Love and Connection
Overwhelmed	Peace and Lightness

This might take some practice to notice the feeling in your body and then evoke a resourced state. It can help to practice doing mindfulness meditation to get more in touch with how energy feels in the body. Try either EFT and/or TRE today to practice letting go of a feeling that you would like to release. Journal about your experience.

Renew, release, let go. Yesterday's gone. There's nothing you can do to bring it back. You can't "should've" done something. You can only DO something. Renew yourself. Release that attachment. Today is a new day!

—Steve Maraboli

Day Fourteen

Today's affirmation: "I am ready and willing to practice being more compassionate towards myself and others. I send loving-kindness to everyone."

Loving-Kindness with Compassion

According to the Merriam-Webster dictionary, the definition of "compassion" is the sympathetic consciousness of others' distress together with a desire to alleviate it. It is about recognizing someone else's suffering and wanting to help.

It is important to cultivate compassion towards others as well as ourselves. When we come from a place of compassion, we not only avoid judging others and ourselves, but we also don't need to hold on to feelings of resentment, shame, guilt, anger, frustration, and hatred. In this way, compassion helps us stay centered and grounded.

This brings up the topic of empathy. Empathy is about really feeling what it is like to be in someone else's shoes. If you were going through a tough time in your life, wouldn't you want to talk to someone who can feel compassion and empathize with your situation?

Today is also about appreciating people just as they are and wishing them well. We all have parts of ourselves that we might not be so proud of and want to hide. Many of us feel we are not smart enough, pretty enough, good enough, likable enough, ambitious enough, etc. We might feel we are too selfish, too bossy, too controlling, too stubborn, etc. One thing we humans are great at is finding fault in others as well as ourselves.

Listen to the audio meditation *Loving-Kindness from a Place of Compassion* to send good vibes to others and yourself. Practicing loving-kindness regularly (also known as "Metta" meditation in Buddhism) can increase a person's capacity for forgiveness, connection to others, self-acceptance, and more. If you are new to this, you might need to practice receiving and giving love. It gets easier the more you do this meditation. During meditation, see if you can send love to the parts of yourself that you want to hide from a place of compassion. This is a good meditation to do whenever you are feeling down or disconnected.

When journaling today, write about the parts of yourself that you want to hide from others and any obstacles you found that might have made this meditation challenging. How did you feel afterwards?

I would like my life to be a statement of love and compassion, and where it isn't that's where my work lies.

—Ram Das

Day Fifteen

Today's affirmation: "I am connected to and give back to my community, offering help to those in need."

Extending Ourselves to Others

Today, reflect on your community. If you don't feel that you are part of a community, what are some ways that you can become part of a community that you feel is in alignment with your values and interests? Volunteering is a great way to offer service and connect with like-minded people.

Consider today as a day of offerings. Offering to be of service to help someone (friend, family member, partner, neighbor, etc.) or doing a nice gesture for another person without expecting anything in return. It could even be about helping a stranger or someone you don't know well. If they offer to reward you in some way, politely decline and suggest instead for them to pay it forward, which can create a chain reaction of raising vibration across the world! It is a lot more powerful when giving an offering to a stranger. It can totally take them by surprise and make their day, while allowing you to practice doing something outside of your comfort zone. Examples are: paying for someone else's beverage when in line at a café, letting someone go ahead of you in line, buying flowers for a stranger or someone you know, carrying something heavy for someone else, etc. The list is endless. If you are physically unable to interact with people in the environment, consider calling someone to offer them emotional support. Journal about how you felt giving of yourself to others.

Day Sixteen

Today's affirmation: "When I forgive myself, it makes it easier to forgive others. I am open and willing to let go of any judgments or negative energy I carry towards others and myself."

Forgiveness

Forgiveness can be a pretty heavy topic. Maybe you feel a little apprehension working on this, which is understandable. However, in order to stay centered and in high vibration, it is important to address the lower vibration stuff that keeps you holding onto judgment, shame, guilt, resentment, anger, disappointment, etc. The person we are really hurting at the end when we don't forgive is ourselves.

This does not mean that forgiving others excuses their actions or that you need to reconcile with that person. It is about releasing the negative energy it created in you. You can forgive and not condone their actions. Use this day as an opportunity to address this topic. Be mindful that if the topic is too heavy for you, and you need more support from a trained professional, such as a psychologist, social worker, or an Internal Family Systems (IFS) therapist, then seek the support you need. In that case, you can skip this day for the time being. If you are interested in working through it now, do the following for others as well as yourself:

1. Take a moment to think about whom you might still be holding a grudge towards. We often have images or conversations come into our mind during the day or night of people we still feel unsettled with. Write their names down and the incident. Also, write down what you need to forgive

yourself for, as you might be holding on to feelings of shame and/or guilt.

2. Think about one person on your list and ask yourself: How has this person's offense negatively impacted my life? Feel how they impacted your life only if it feels safe to do so. If it is a trauma, for example, I suggest doing this with a professional. Otherwise, notice where it feels in your body and just be with that feeling.

3. Then, to help you forgive this person (or yourself), ask the following questions:

- What might have that person been going through emotionally at the time?

- What could he/she have used or needed to have reacted differently?

- Was this person reacting out of feeling hurt?

- What was he/she like as a child?

- Then ask yourself, how have you learned and grown from that experience?

4. Make the decision to forgive (which again does not necessarily mean you are condoning the action).

5. Listen to the audio *Loving-Kindness from a Place of Compassion* to send blessings to that person and yourself.

If the energy does not feel fully released, you can also say the *Ho'oponopono (ho-o-pono-pono) prayer*, an ancient prayer that came from Hawaii, if it feels right for your situation. It has four parts to it. Repeat the following phrase several times while holding the image of the person or yourself in mind and feeling into the energy that needs to be released. Remember that you are doing this for yourself to have a peace of mind:

I'm sorry.
Please forgive me.
My intentions are good. (optional)
Thank you.
I love you.

There are different ways to interpret its meaning. This is the way I suggest interpreting it: The "I'm sorry" is about taking responsibility for your thoughts since you created them. The "please forgive me" is about asking the person or yourself for forgiveness (this still does not mean you are condoning the particular action). I like to add "my intentions are good" to really help absolve any feelings of guilt you might be harboring. "Thank you" is about appreciation for allowing the release of this energy, and "I love you" is about sending good energy to yourself or the person. This prayer can be profoundly healing. There are even song versions of it. I like *Ho'oponopono* by Jennifer Zulli from the album *Goddess Rising*.

Day Seventeen

Today's affirmation: "I feel into the peace that is at the core of my being and know I can access it with every breath I take."

I Am at Peace

Today is about feeling the energy of peace. Listen to the audio meditation *I Am Peace* and try to take this energy with you throughout the day, repeating the affirmation above as often as you remember.

List all the places that bring you peace. What do you enjoy doing that helps bring up this energy? What does it feel like in your body when you are at peace? Notice how you might be breathing more fully and deeply. I like to bring to mind a light feather blowing in the wind as I feel into my body. Pick something to do today that elicits the feeling of peace within you. If you can, also choose the environment from one of the places you listed. You can journal about your experience and anything that comes up for you today.

Day Eighteen

Today's affirmation: "I approve of myself and am worthy of love and happiness."

Sending Love to Myself

Today is a day to bask in love. What does a day of self-love look like for you? I suggest writing a love letter to yourself. You can either write a letter or a card, decorating the front, and bringing out your inner child. You can add words on the front that you can use for your journey in life—like strength, forgiveness, trust, etc. During the writing section, address the letter or card to yourself. The following is just an example if you need help to get you started:

Dear _____,

I congratulate you for _____.

I love so many things about you! You are (all positive words)
_____.

I forgive you for (only add this if you feel the need to forgive yourself) _____.

You are doing a such a great job with _____.

I know you have had obstacles in your life, but you got through them and they have made you stronger.

My wish for you is _____.

You get the idea. You can imagine you are the wise older version of yourself, sending yourself a letter of love and appreciation. If you choose, you can give yourself supportive advice. Feel into what you would like to hear. Enjoy this exercise. However, it can also bring up tender emotions. It is a good idea to do self-nurturing things today like take a bath by candlelight, get a massage, do your nails, buy yourself flowers, watch a funny movie, etc.

After you write your letter or card, put it in an envelope and mail it to yourself. I would suggest waiting a month before mailing it out, so it will sound fresh and new. You can also give it to someone else (sealed up) and have them mail it to you in a month or so. You can come back to this page and journal about what it felt like to open the letter and read what you wrote to yourself.

How you love yourself is how you teach others to love you.

—Rupi Kaur

Day Nineteen

Today's affirmation: "By connecting from my heart, I listen with compassion to others when they share their stories while expressing myself in an authentic way."

Mindful Connection

Today is about having the intention to really embody the affirmation above. Part of staying in high vibration involves our connection to others. When we feel heard and validated for how we are feeling and are fully present and engaged in conversation, our emotional connection with others is strengthened. Deep, meaningful connections have a huge impact on our happiness.

Michael Sorensen is the author of the book *I Hear You* that explores validation and how to empathize with someone in a conversation. Some examples of validation are: *It makes sense that you feel or think... it sounds as though you are feeling... I hear you saying...* It is also important to communicate in an authentic way on your end. This means talking in an honest yet caring way about how you think and feel so that you can honor your feelings. If you are looking for more connection, you might consider looking into joining in-person Meetup groups (Meetup.com) and/or online authentic relating communities, such as *Get Back to Life* (GetBackToLife.org), *The Connection Movement* (TheConnectionMovement.com), *Authentic Revolution* (AuthRev.org), *Let's Be Authentic* (LetsBeAuthentic.com), etc. There are also courses and books on the topic of meaningful communication that can be explored further. The following are some resources:

- *The Power of Validation* by Karyn Hall and Melissa Cook

- *Genuine Validation: Compassionate Communication that Transforms Difficult Relationships at Home and Work* by Corinne Stoewsand

- *Nonviolent Communication* by Marshal Rosenberg

- *Circling and Authentic Relating Practice Guide* by Marc Beneteau

Today is about connecting with a friend, family member, or partner with the above affirmation in mind. Have the intention of being fully present, which means avoiding all multitasking. Ask them how they are doing and really listen to their story from a place of compassion and empathy. Work on also being comfortable with some silence instead of talking right away. Journal about your experience and any insights that you had.

Connection gives purpose and meaning to our lives.

—Brene Brown

Day Twenty

Today's affirmation: "I choose to be positive and be in my joy."

I Am in My Joy

Today, we will explore the feeling of joy. Joy is one of the highest vibrations. There was a longitudinal analysis done on the happiness of about 5,000 people over the span of 20 years (from 1983-2003) to study its impact through social networks. The study found that happiness seems to create a domino effect; those who interact with happy people are likely to become happier in the near future, and this chain reaction has been observed up to three degrees of separation (e.g., the friends of one's friends' friends).[4]

Dr. Hawkins discusses the scale of consciousness that he developed in the book *Power vs. Force*. This scale spans from 0 -1000 Hz, where 700 -1000 represents enlightenment and below 200 represents the vibrational frequencies of emotions like shame, guilt, and apathy. From his research, he found that emotions below 200 weaken the body, and emotions above 200 strengthen the body. According to Dr. Hawkins, measuring at a frequency of 500 or above is pure unconditional love, where we are in total harmony with ourselves and our environment. Joy measures at 540 Hz according to his scale. Let's raise our vibration today!

Listen to the meditation *I Am Joy*. Your goal is to carry this feeling of joy throughout the day while focusing on entertaining only positive thoughts. You might want to avoid watching the news, sad movies, or talking about things that spark lower vibrational thinking to help you stay in your state of joy. Instead, consider playing uplifting music that helps conjure up this feeling. I like to listen to the following songs: *I'm So Excited* by the Pointer Sisters, *Holiday* by Madonna, *Walking on Sunshine* by Katrina and the Waves, and *Happy* by Pharrell Williams. You can sing and/or dance along! You might want to make a "joy" playlist. Journal about your experience today with the following questions in mind:

- How hard or easy was it to stay in the state of joy?

- Was your mind trying to bring you back to lower vibrational thinking?

- How can you add more joy into your life? What action steps can you take?

- What things/activities bring you joy?

Have this list handy when you need a pick-me-up. I like to call them *joy lifters* (for example, self-pampering activities, listening to uplifting music, calling a friend, dancing, singing, watching a comedy, dressing up, etc.).

The joy we feel has little to do with the circumstances of our lives and everything to do with the focus of our lives.

—Russel M. Nelson

Day Twenty-one

Today's affirmation: "I choose to have fun with
myself exploring new adventures."

I Enjoy Being with Myself

Today is a day of exploration and adventure as you think about a new hobby you might want to try. If you prefer, you can make time for an existing hobby that you enjoy. A hobby can be anything from learning a new language (for example, using the free app called *Duolingo*), taking a dance lesson, painting, learning a musical instrument, taking up gardening, knitting, learning a sport, joining a book club, writing, etc. It's endless. List your interests and/or hobbies and what you would enjoy exploring. Most importantly, have fun with it!

Day Twenty-two

Today's affirmation: "I intend to release my old beliefs and stories, and in so doing, I am allowing myself to be open to experience my potential from a place of an empowered self."

My New Story

Today is about letting go of the old stories that don't serve you. To get to a high vibrational state, it is important to acknowledge and let go of the stories that have been keeping you in a low vibrational state.

Stories come from our past experiences; we see life through a lens of things that happened to us long ago. They may not be relevant at all to what is actually happening in the now! For instance, you might be telling yourself that you don't have the talent to be a successful writer because your freshman English professor told you so, or that you will never find a life partner because you've had a succession of failed relationships.

Perhaps you believe that your problems and unhappiness in life exist due to life circumstances—things that are happening *to* you—which allows you to release all responsibilities to your state of happiness. This is an example of how we might be giving away our power. It is much more empowering to take responsibility for our suffering so that we can do something about it. Staying in a victim role does not offer that.

This is not to minimize that many unfortunate things happen in life that are also beyond our control, like death or getting laid off from a job you loved because of the economy, for example. You might not be able to control circumstances, but "responsibility" can be defined as our ability to respond in an empowered way. Here are five steps to help release the old and welcome new beliefs that are empowering:

1. **Write down the old story or belief.** Write down your story or belief you are ready to let go of on a piece of paper and then read it out loud.

2. **Honor & respect it.** Take a moment to honor and respect your story or belief. If there is any pain or any other uncomfortable feelings that come up, take some time to feel them from a place of compassion.

3. **Do a releasing ritual.** Then tear up the old story in small pieces. Do the audio *Breathwork* and imagine letting go of the story through a fast breathing sequence; then bring in peace and loving energy during the deep breathing section.

4. **State your intention.** Say to yourself, *"I no longer need this story. I choose to let go of any attachments to this story that have kept me down, for I no longer need it to define me. Whenever I notice this story come up, I am going to gently remind myself, 'No, I have a new story and belief' and then shift my attention onto something else."*

5. **Write your new story or belief.** Write down your new story from an empowered self and remind yourself of this new belief or story whenever the old story or belief resurfaces.

6. **Do the Circle of Potential.** Do the *Circle of Potential* exercise that we did on Day One:

> Start in a standing position. Imagine you are drawing a circle in front of you. In that circle is this new you, feeling empowered and happy with the new story or belief. Notice your posture, your facial expression, and how you are feeling inside your body. Now step inside this circle. Close your eyes and feel all the sensations in your body from the top of your head down to the bottom of your feet. Stand with similar posture and facial expression. Stay in this space for a couple of minutes. Afterwards, write down your new story.

Day Twenty-three

Today's affirmation: "I live my life with awareness and gratitude no matter my circumstances."

Gratitude

Today, we will focus on gratitude. Off the top of your head, what are you feeling grateful for in your life? Can you name at least four things? Gratitude is one of the fastest ways to raise our vibration. Life coach, Tony Robbins, posted on his Facebook page, "The antidote to fear is gratitude. The antidote to anger is gratitude. You can't feel fear or anger while feeling gratitude at the same time."

Having a positive attitude and being grateful for everything you have in your life will not only make your life feel lighter and more pleasant, but it will also raise your vibration and, therefore, help attract more positive people and opportunities to you. Writers like Napoleon Hill, Deepak Chopra, Wayne Dyer, Rhonda Byrne, and many others, discuss the benefits of bringing yourself to a high vibrational state. As we discussed on Day 20, the happiness study revealed that living in the high vibrational state of happiness can also produce a chain reaction and affect so many people's lives!

Today, we will play the *Hunt for Gratitude* game to raise our vibration. This game is even more fun if played with someone else. I encourage you to ask a partner or a friend to join you. Starting from the morning, your job is to find as many things as you can that you are grateful or thankful for throughout the day and jot them down. Here are some ideas:

a sunny day, yummy breakfast, good night's sleep, little traffic, getting a parking spot easily, seeing a smile on someone's face, a phone call from a friend, a compliment, etc. You get the idea. If you are playing with someone else, both of you should jot things down separately.

The goal of the game is to find as many things as possible. The person who finds the most things that they feel grateful for in the day wins the game. You can even create a reward that the winner gets. Maybe a reward could be dinner made just for you or ordering out? A massage, a bouquet of flowers, or anything else that would feel good.

Journal about how today's experience felt in your body. Did you notice if your vibration amped up as the day went on, finding things to feel grateful for? In general, I suggest keeping a daily gratitude journal and/or having a gratitude buddy who you can express what you are feeling grateful for every day.

Be thankful for what you have; you'll end up having more. If you concentrate on what you don't have, you will never, ever have enough.

—Oprah Winfrey

Day Twenty-four

Today's affirmation: "I live from a place of an empowered self. I speak my truth and honor my values."

I Am Empowered

Today is about feeling into an empowered self. When you step into your power, what does that look and feel like? Think about your role models and list them.

- What is it about them that make them special to you?

- Do you find them all empowered with a strong sense of self?

- Do they speak their truth and stand by their values?

- Do they carry any particular values that have inspired you on your life's journey?

Write about the attributes they possess that contribute to their power and strong sense of self-worth. What do they look like and sound like? Even though we did the *Circle of Potential* exercise previously, it is important to really get this concept of self-empowerment, so I invite you to do it again today:

Start in a standing position. Imagine you are drawing a circle in front of you. In that circle is an empowered you with a strong sense of identity and self-worth. Notice your posture, your facial expression, and how you are feeling inside your body. Really feel into all your senses. Now step inside this circle. Close your eyes and feel all the sensations in your body from the top of your head down to the bottom of your feet. Stand with similar posture and facial expression. Stay in this space for a couple of minutes.

Repeat today's affirmation throughout the day. Write down your values and what it means for you to live from an empowered self.

Make your life a masterpiece; imagine no limitations on what you can be, have, or do.

—Brian Tracy

Day Twenty-five

Today's affirmation: "My immune system is strong, resilient, and functions optimally."

Resilient Immune System

Bruce Lipton, a cell biologist in the field of Epigenetics, discusses just how much power we have to override our genes in his book *The Biology of Belief.* He conducted a study using stem cells. He isolated one stem cell, put it in a Petri dish, and allowed it to divide into many cells. They were all genetically identical since they came from one cell. He then separated the cells into three Petri dishes; each dish was comprised of a different environment. Even though each dish contained the same genetic cell, because the environment was different in each dish, the cells formed into different components. In the first dish they formed bone, in the second they formed muscle, and in the third they formed fat cells. He concluded that the environment actually controls the fate of a cell.

A study conducted at Massachusetts General Hospital (MGH) evaluated mind/body techniques and their impact on genetic expression. The study found that practices like meditation, yoga, deep breathing, and prayer, which are used to induce deep rest, produce positive immediate changes in the expression of genes connected to immune function, energy production, and insulin secretion. Conversely, holding on to emotions, such as fear, anger, resentment, grief, and hatred, provides an underlying basis for creating chronic stress behaviors and activating disease.[5]

Even though we are all born with a particular genetic expression, these studies reinforce the concept that genes still need to be turned on by their environment. Science also cannot explain some of the spontaneous remissions that have occurred with various diseases, including cancer. This brings up the notion of just how powerful our minds are. I do not believe, though, that just thinking positive thoughts leads to physical cures. Make sure to consult your doctor or medical practitioner if you are having health issues. I do believe cures are possible, but it is first important to let go of the lower level vibrational emotions that are stuck in the body, like the ones mentioned above. Then, thinking positively, visualizing, and really feeling into high vibrational energy throughout your body as if you are already living from that place of being healed, can be transformational. In my practice, I have seen a remarkable improvement in health following this technique.

Today, listen to the audio *My Resilient Immune System* and really feel into your immune system's strength and power. Journal about your experience with today's meditation.

Your brain and body have never been separate and the bridge between them is your immune system.

—Dr. Dispenza

Day Twenty-six

Today's affirmation: "I aspire to live in balance. My intention is to notice my energetic state and provide what it needs to bring me back to my center."

Chakra Balancing

The word *chakra* comes from the Indian language Sanskrit, and it means vortex, spinning wheel, or circle. The belief is that chakras are circles of energy or energy centers, flowing through the center of our body from the base of the spine to the top of the head (in our spiritual body that surrounds our physical body). They assist in the running of our body, mind, and soul. According to this philosophy, if there is energy blockage in a chakra and the energy is not flowing well, it could have a negative impact on our physical health, mental health, and spirit.

Today, listen to the audio *Chakra Balancing* and follow the guidance provided. Certain chakras might trigger tender emotions. Be open to feeling anything that might come up from a place of compassion. Journal about what this experience was like and anything else you might want to process.

Day Twenty-seven

Today's affirmation: "I choose to believe that there are no mistakes in life, just experiences. No matter where I am on my path, I know I am learning and growing, and have faith that everything will be ok."

Connecting to the Universe

Consider today's affirmation. It might be difficult at times to see mistakes made in life as experiences that we learn and grow from. If you choose to hold on to believing people make mistakes, that is fine too. However, notice how much resistance you might be feeling in your body when you hold on to the idea that you made a mistake versus seeing it as an experience that you learned from; how much more accepting and forgiving you might be towards yourself and others if you see life through the lens that everything is an experience.

This brings up the topic of faith. Faith, no matter what your religious or spiritual background, can be a powerful force that provides support and strength to get through tough times. One of the best ways to transcend the feeling of gloom and doom is to have faith; believing that the universe (or God, or loving energy, or whatever works for you) wants the best for you and knowing that no matter what, everything will be ok. Even if you currently can't see exactly how it will all work out, faith can help keep us stay centered. In order to create more peace in our lives during a time of crisis, we have got to *feel* it.

Meditation is one of the best ways that can help to conjure up this feeling of an ever-loving presence that resides deep inside of us and all around us. Today, listen to the audio *I Am Peace,* or *I Am Joy* to help you connect to your faith.

Day Twenty-eight

Today's affirmation: "I incorporate playfulness into my life because laughter and silliness bring me joy and a sense of lightness."

Playfulness

Today is about bringing out the inner child in you. Think back to yourself as a child and conjure up a memory when you felt silly and playful (or if childhood brings up too many unhappy memories think back to a time later in life you remember feeling playful and silly). What were you doing in this scene? How did others react around you? Notice your mannerisms and how you remember feeling inside. Were you laughing during this time and feeling light and spacious? If this is too difficult for you, and you don't remember a time, then think about a person whom you find silly and playful. It could even be a celebrity like Jim Carrey or Will Ferrell. What might it feel like to be silly like them? Write about some of these experiences and feel into the lightness and joy. Today is about bringing out the inner child in you to be playful and silly. Some ideas are:

- Playing a game like Pictionary, Apples to Apples, or Twister with someone

- Putting on a totally mismatched, ridiculous outfit that will bring out the giggles in you

- Doing something outrageous with your hair

- Wearing a costume, funny glasses or hat that bring out the giggles

- Watching a funny movie with friends and having a costume party

- Doing Mad Libs

- Taking a laughter yoga class

- Expressing playfulness through dance

- Rolling around in the grass or running through leaves and kicking them up in the air (depending on the season of course).

What are some other ideas that tickle your fancy?

A playful path is the shortest road to happiness.

—Bernie Dekoven

Day Twenty-nine

Today's affirmation: "My dreams can turn into reality. My intention is to live in the vibration as if my dreams already came true."

Positive Envisioning

We are powerful beings. Do you know that our minds don't know the difference between reality and imagery? In other words, the mind thinks that what you are imagining is actually happening. As an NLP practitioner, I often help clients manipulate their minds with the images they create to help them achieve their goals or desires.

In 1967, a famous study conducted in Australia by psychologist Dr. Allen Richardson proves the power of visualization. He chose students at random, who had never practiced visualization, to play basketball. He split them into three groups and tested how many free throws they could make. The first group practiced free throws every day for twenty days. The second group made free throws on the first day and the twentieth day, as did the third group. But participants of the third group spent 20 minutes every day visualizing free throws. If they "missed," they "practiced" getting the next shot right using their senses. On the twentieth day, Richardson measured the percentage of improvement in each group. The group that practiced daily improved by 24 percent. The second group, unsurprisingly, did not improve at all. The third group, which had physically practiced no more than the second but incorporated visualization, did 23 percent better—almost as good as the first group.[6]

This study shows the power of daily practice in visualization! The way they did it was not just seeing the ball go into the net but really putting themselves on the court in their mind's eye with all their senses: feeling the ball as it launches out of their hands, hearing the swoosh of the net. So, imagine what will happen if you do this kind of visualization around what you want to be manifested! What I find even more powerful is when we imagine and talk about the desire as if it already happened. In my opinion, using the past tense helps to convince the unconscious mind that this new reality is possible.

Today, journal about what you want to manifest. Then call up a friend to tell them about how you want to practice this envisioning exercise and talk to them about your new future vision as if it already happened. You can fast forward to several months, a year, or several years from now and talk about it looking back. You can mix past and present tenses. Feel into your senses in the imagery, how amazing you felt in your body, and if there are others around you, how great they felt too. Here is an example if you are about to go on a job interview:

OMG! You won't believe it! I was called in for an interview, and it went so well! I felt confident speaking. I knew all the answers to the questions that the interviewer asked. We even laughed a lot, and he told me I got the job! He even offered a salary even higher than expected! "Then you can fast forward again... "OMG, I love my job!!! I love the coworkers that I am working with. We have been going out after work. The job has been so stimulating and rewarding! I am so happy I am working here.

Notice the first part of the imagery used past tense, and the second part incorporated other tenses as well. Play with the tenses. The most important thing is that it's about really *feeling* it in your body while you are talking. Practicing this exercise with someone helps to bring it to life.

Day Thirty

Today's affirmation: "I appreciate myself for all that I have learned, who I have become, and how I continue to evolve."

Appreciation

Congratulations! You did it!!! You took the challenge and got through it! Yay! Woohoo! Today is about appreciating YOU. Really feel into the affirmation above. During journaling today, reflect on what you have learned through this program about yourself.

- How can you take the aspects of the program to continue helping you stay centered, grounded, and in high vibration?

- What can you incorporate into your daily routine?

- When can you make time for it or them?

I highly recommend doing the *Circle of Potential* exercise every morning and at least one meditation daily. Take a moment to visualize your future day, incorporating all the things you want to add into your life. You might consider making a schedule of a sample day and what that would like. I encourage you to reward yourself for sticking with the program and finishing it. Give yourself the certificate that is attached to the back of this book. You deserve it! Some ideas for additional rewards are:

- Buying yourself flowers or something else special

- Treating yourself to a massage

- Treating yourself to a warm bath with candlelight and music

BEYOND THE 30 DAYS

I truly hope you enjoyed doing this challenge and that it will continue to help you in years to come. You can go back and do the challenge again, maybe spending more time on each theme. You could also go back and just keep the affirmation of each day in mind and do the meditations. You could go back and pick a section at a time to focus on or feel into what you need that day. Let your inner guidance be your compass. Overall, I hope this challenge will help you embrace life in a lighter way. The tools and exercises offered can help us to surrender (letting go of resistance) to whatever life brings us without attaching to any particular outcome.

If you enjoyed doing this challenge, please consider writing a review. This helps others discover the book! If you would like more support on your journey, feel free to contact me through my website:

HolisticWellnessNY.com

I offer individualized life coaching and nutrition counseling to support you in manifesting your goals. I incorporate tools, such as hypnosis, NLP, and energy work to get effective results. Wishing you many more years of staying grounded, centered, and in high vibration!

Warmly,
Ilona Yukov

CERTIFICATE FOR COMPLETING THE
30-DAY HIGH VIBE CHALLENGE

this certificate is awarded to:

_____

in recognition of

your effort in staying grounded, centered and in
high vibration

_____   _____

Signature   Date

APPENDIX

A Guide for the Audio:
Parts from a Place of Compassion

Inner parts work can be a very powerful process, and it can be a little complicated. There are different ways people practice parts work. The following guide is how I like to practice it. Here are some guidelines to help you have a deeper, more meaningful experience.

In parts work, you scan your body to feel what area wants your attention most and the predominant emotion coming up for you there. You want to notice the qualities of the sensations there. Then you want to get curious about the emotion connected to those sensations to give that part a voice.

When we work with different parts of ourselves, it is helpful to use the phrase, "something in me feels this way" —so as not to identify with the parts of you. You are taking on the role of the observer. As the observer, you start having an inward conversation with a part of you from a non-judgmental and compassionate place. Your job is to get better acquainted with the different parts of you and strengthen your relationship with them, so they don't take over how you behave and act. In essence, you are the container of all your parts—the sum of all your parts. For example, we can have an anxious part that might want to avoid going to a particular engagement. All parts, no matter how they react, are trying to protect us in their own way, even if the way they are protecting us seems irrational. In this example, we can acknowledge this part of us but then make our own decision whether we want to avoid the event that is making this part anxious or not. It allows us to make decisions from an empowered place.

Something to keep in mind is that as you pay attention to one part, another part can come up, wanting to express a different feeling. Maybe there is another part that feels excited about going to the same event. Notice that part too. All parts of you have a right to exist and feel whatever comes up for them. You are there to witness and acknowledge all the parts that want your attention from a place of compassion and empathy.

Often, these parts just want you to be with them and want to be heard. That alone can help them get back to feeling calm and centered. Sometimes, they might give you a directive. In a sense, you're having a conversation with a part of you as if it is another human being. This helps not to identify with it. You can imagine a part of you as a friend that comes to you for support or needing assistance. Because you are working on developing a close relationship with the parts of you, it helps to say, "I hear you." This lets the part know that it is heard. Asking, "Did I understand that right?" helps to make sure you understand its perspective. Often, the parts that come up are younger than you. An earlier memory from childhood can trigger the emotion that you are experiencing when doing parts work. As the observer, you are acting as the older, wiser adult, providing this younger part nurturance and support. It might want to be hugged or picked up like a child. You can imagine that is what you are doing to provide it comfort. You can use gestures like hugging yourself and/or placing your hand on your heart. You can also ask this part 'what would it like to be called?" A "he," "she" or "it"? You can even ask how old this part is, which helps to dis-identify with it even more while still supporting it with compassion.

Because you are the older, wiser adult and the container of all your parts, you can offer it a different perspective to help shift how it is feeling. It is especially powerful when you find evidence that challenges what it is believing. All people are loveable and good enough. We are all worthy of happiness, and we learn from our experiences. Parts work can really allow us not to identify with our minds and the thoughts and images that it creates. Its main purpose is to give all parts a voice, so they feel heard to bring us to a place of inner peace and harmony.

BIBLIOGRAPHY

Cornell, Ann W (1996). *The Power of Focusing: A Practical Guide to Emotional Self-Healing.* California: New Harbinger Publications

Dispenza, Joe (2007). *Evolve Your Brain.* Florida: Health Communications, Inc.

Hawkins, David (2012). *Power vs. Force.* California: Hay House, Inc.

Katie, Byron and Mitchell, Stephen (2002). *Loving What Is.* New York: Three Rivers Press

Lipton, Bruce H (2016). *The Biology of Belief.* California: Hay House, Inc.

Sorensen, Michael S (2017). *I Hear You.* Pennsylvania: Autumn Creek Press

Tolle, Eckhart (1999). *The Power of Now.* California: Namaste Publishing and New World Library

ENDNOTES

1   Yano, Jessica M. and Yu, Kristie and Donaldson, Gregory P. and Shastri, Gauri G. and Ann, Phoebe and Ma, Liang and Nagler, Cathryn R. and Ismagilov, Rustem F. and Mazmanian, Sarkis K. and Hsiao, Elaine Y (2015). *Indigenous Bacteria from the Gut Microbiota Regulate Host Serotonin Biosynthesis.* Cell, 161 (2). p 264

2   Blumenthal, James A (2007). *Exercise and Pharmacotherapy in the Treatment of Major Depressive Disorder.* Journal of Psychosomatic Medicine, Volume 69 – Issue 7 – Page 587-596

3   Levitin, Daniel J (2015). *Why the Modern World is Bad for Your Brain.* The Guardian, Jan. 18

4   Fowler, James H. and Christakis, Nicholas A (2008). *Dynamic Spread of Happiness in a Large Social Network: Longitudinal Analysis over 20 years in the Framingham Heart Study.* British Medical Journal, December 4

5   Bhasin, Mlk., J. A. Dusek, et al (2013). *Relaxation Response Induces Temporal Transcriptome Changes in*

Energy Metabolism, Insulin Secretion and Inflammatory Pathways. PLOS ONE 8 (5): e62817

6   Richardson, Allen (1967). *Mental Practice: A Review and Discussion (Parts 1 and 2).* Research Quarterly, 38, (1) pp. 95–107, (2) pp. 263–273

RESOURCES

Books

The Power of Validation by Karyn Hall and Melissa Cook
Genuine Validation: Compassionate Communication that Transforms Difficult Relationships at Home and Work by Corinne Stoewsand
Nonviolent Communication by Marshal Rosenberg
Circling and Authentic Relating Practice Guide by Marc Beneteau
The Power of Focusing: A Practical Guide to Emotional Self-Healing by Ann Weiser Cornell

EFT

The Tapping Solution: A Revolutionary System for Stress-Free Living by Nick Ortner and Mark Hyman M.D
App – The Tapping Solution
TheTappingSolution.com

Online Communities

GetBackToLife.org
TheConnectionMovement.com
Meetup.com
AuthRev.org
LetsBeAuthentic.com

Songs

I'm So Excited by the Pointer Sisters
Holiday by Madonna
Walking on Sunshine by Katrina and the Waves
Happy by Pharrell Williams
Ho'oponopono by Jennifer Zulli

ACKNOWLEDGMENTS

To my dear friend and editor, Laurie Hefner, who did an amazing job editing this book. I couldn't have done it without you!

To my dear friend and mentor, Valerie Greene, who provided feedback for this book. I feel so grateful having you in my life.

To my parents for their love and support throughout the years. Thanks mom and dad for always believing in me.

To my beloved Tony, who has been encouraging me to write and offers so much loving-kindness. I appreciate all that you contributed in the making of the audios and helping me with the finishing touches of this book.

I also would not have been able to create this book if it was not for my teachers, clients, and friends from whom I gained valuable insight over the years. Many thanks to all of you.

ABOUT THE AUTHOR

Ilona Yukov founded Holistic Wellness, NY, a private practice, whose aim is to help people achieve their health and wellness goals. She has over 20 years of experience working with clients with various conditions.

Ilona graduated with an M.A. in occupational therapy from New York University in 1998. She continued her studies and received her training as a holistic health coach from the Institute of Integrative Nutrition in 2003. She went on to study various mind/body techniques, such as mindfulness, Reiki, Emotional Freedom Technique (EFT), breathwork, and guided imagery. She also became certified as a Neuro-Linguistic Programming (NLP) Practitioner, graduating from the International Center for Positive Change & Hypnosis in New York City. She further received training in hypnosis by the renowned hypnotist, Melissa Tiers, at The Center for Integrative Hypnosis. Her experience working as an occupational therapist in a hospital, nursing home, and school setting gave her skills to work with people of diverse backgrounds, ages, and health conditions. In 2008, Ilona published an article on how food can affect the behavior of children with special needs. Presently, she is working in an elementary school with children with disabilities as an occupational therapist and provides wellness services for adults in her private practice. Her mission is to empower, guide, and support people in turning their desires into reality. She provides life coaching, nutrition counseling, NLP, hypnosis, and energy healing via video and phone throughout the United States.

Information about all of the author's coaching services—and a way to contact the author—can be found at the following website: HolisticWellnessNy.com.